Doctor Owlkin and The H.O.M.E. Team
*(**H**elp **O**r **M**otivate Everybody!)*

Celebrating Our Differences and Diversity with Inclusion

Our Mission: The Doctor Owlkin book series was created *to raise the self-esteem and confidence of children with special needs, disabilities, or differences and teach other children acceptance and inclusion of those with differences or disabilities*. Even though others may be "different," we find that inside everybody just wants to be loved, encouraged, accepted, appreciated, and included!

Doctor Owlkin, the members of The H.O.M.E. Team, and the animal characters in the books become the heroes who find a way to make their diversity or differences an attribute or advantage. The H.O.M.E. Team is led by wise old **Doctor Owlkin** and loving **Nurse Sharky**, who bring together their helpers. The first four books in the series tell the amazing stories of each of the helpers. The H.O.M.E. Team includes **Trouble**, a Bloodhound who was born with extraordinarily long and useful ears; **King Tux**, a tiny cat who has a BIG personality and smarts; **Pirate**, a lop-eared rabbit with only one eye who sees the world in a unique way; and **Goldie**, a Golden Retriever who was born with 3 ½ legs but doesn't let that stop her from being a hero. Each of these characters has adapted and developed special skills – their "superpowers" – that allow them to uplift and encourage others to be the best they can be, regardless of their differences!

In subsequent books, The H.O.M.E. Team goes out into the community to help other animals. Each book addresses a new "difference" to teach children why that character is special, and that we are all "different and unique" in some way.

As **Doctor Owlkin** always reminds the team, **"It's WHOOOOOO you are on the inside that matters most!"**

Dedicated in loving memory of
Laxmi Devi Agusala and Ike Perlman

Edited by Gary M. Hardee, PhD
Consultant: Annalise Sansouci, CCLS

Website – www.HelpOrMotivateEverybody.org

Facebook – https://www.facebook.com/DrOwlkin

YouTube – https://www.youtube.com/watch?v=mTV7h_BXjEU

Instagram – https://www.instagram.com/dr.owlkin/?hl=en

Twitter – https://twitter.com/TheHOMETeamHel1

Linkedin – https://www.linkedin.com/company/help-or-motivate-everybody

ISBN: 978-1-7368708-1-5
1st Edition

Every picture has a hidden heart, can you find it?

Mr. Grumps clomps into the Hopeville shelter.
His heavy footsteps sound very loud.

CLOMP CLOMP CLOMP!

"Well, hello, Mr. Grumps," Miss Peeps,
the receptionist, chirps brightly. "What brings you in?"

Mr. Grumps frowns. He always frowns.

"Those darn cats keep running away from my farm,"
Mr. Grumps grumbles. "I need to adopt another one."

"Well, we have one cat left," Miss Peeps says.
"He's very small, but oh so smart."

Mr. Grumps huffs, "Let's see him!"

In the corner of a big cage sits a tiny cat.
He is about the size of a groundhog and
the big cage makes him look even smaller.

He has shiny black fur that wraps around a V-shaped white satin
neck. His tiny white front paws look like cotton gloves. His tiny rear
paws are white sneakers.

"He looks like he's wearing a tuxedo!" says Mr. Grumps.

"Oh, yes, he does," Miss Peep tweets. "Hey, you could call him Tux!"

Mr. Grumps just harrumphs.

Tiny Tux indeed looks ready for a formal affair.

But Tux has never been anywhere outside of the shelter.
He was the smallest cat born in the litter.
All of the other cats were adopted.

Nobody wanted to adopt Tux.

"I don't think this runt can scare away the mice on my farm," Mr. Grumps snorts. "But if he's the only one you have, I guess I'll have to give him a try."

Tux looks at Mr. Grumps closely.
He's heard about Mr. Grumps and
doesn't want to go with him.

Tux twists his head from side to side.
He does that when he is thinking.

He is planning his escape from Miss Peeps but she sweeps him into a carrier before he can do anything about it!

After a long ride, Mr. Grumps finally stops his truck. He grabs the carrier, knocking Tux into the side of it. As he walks toward the barn he gives Tux a mean look and snaps at him!

"Okay, runt, we're here. Your job is to keep those mice out of the barn. They scare my horses, and I can't have that," Mr. Grumps snarls.

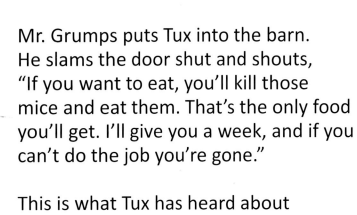

Mr. Grumps puts Tux into the barn. He slams the door shut and shouts, "If you want to eat, you'll kill those mice and eat them. That's the only food you'll get. I'll give you a week, and if you can't do the job you're gone."

This is what Tux has heard about Mr. Grumps from other cats in the shelter.

Mr. Grumps is an unpleasant fellow.

Tux looks around the big barn.
He is surprised to see he isn't alone.
A pair of white whiskers is trying to hide behind a bale of hay.

Slowly an orange cat with white and black markings
comes out from behind the bale of hay.

"Hi," Tux says with a friendly meow. "What's your name?"

"I'm Scooter," the barn cat replies.

Scooter looks nervously around the barn.

"I am so sorry Mr. Grumps brought you here," Scooter says. "This is
a terrible place to live."

Scooter is the only cat left in the barn.
All of the others have run away.
Scooter tells Tux he also ran away.
Mr. Grumps tried to stop him.

He shot at him with a BB gun.

"Oh my!" Tux exclaims.

A neighbor lady took Scooter in, but
Mr. Grumps found him. Then he put a tracker on his collar.

"I don't like killing the mice," Scooter says. "The neighbor lady sneaks food over to me so I can just chase the mice away. But they keep coming back. That makes Mr. Grumps mad. So, I hide."

Tux tells Scooter he doesn't want to kill mice either. "It just doesn't feel right," Tux says.

Tux stands next to Scooter, twisting his head from side to side. Tux is thinking. *What to do? What to do?...*

Tux hears the horses suddenly rear.
They raise their legs into the air and neigh loudly.
Then Tux hears a rustling sound in the haystacks.

"A mouse!" Scooter whispers.

Tux jumps to his feet and runs over to talk to the horses.
"Shh," Tux says, waving his white cotton paws.
"Calm down. It's going to be all right."

To Scooter's surprise, the horses calm down.
They seem to trust Tux.

Tux quietly moves
toward the haystack.

He sees that the mouse
is making a nest.

Tux paces in circles like cats like to do.
He turns his head side to side. He is thinking again.
Then his eyes light up!

"I have an idea," Tux whispers to Scooter.
"First, let's get your collar off so
Mr. Grumps doesn't know where you are."

Because Tux has tiny paws, he is able to slip them under Scooter's collar.

Tux pulls and tugs, then pushes and twists some more. Finally, the collar snaps. Scooter smiles.

Tux tells Scooter, "Here's what we're going to do..."

Tux explains his plan. He figures out that the mice don't mean to scare the horses. They just want a comfortable place to live.

"We're going to find a place where they can build a mouse village," Tux says. "Then they won't come to the barn and bother Mr. Grumps' horses."

Tux smiles. "And Scooter, you can go live with
the nice neighbor lady." Scooter gets very excited at
this idea and exclaims. "That is a fantastic idea!
You're so smart! You may be tiny but you think like a King."

Tux beams. He stands as tall as he can puffing out
his white satin chest, his tiny cotton paws on his hips.

"Hmmm. I like that," he says.
"You can call me King Tux from now on!"

Then with a dash, the newly crowned King Tux
and Scooter scurry around the barn, looking for
a way out. Scooter finds a hole in the wall.

It is too tiny for him, but not for King Tux.
With Scooter's help, King Tux squeezes through the hole.

Outside, King Tux hears
Mr. Grumps' footsteps.
CLOMP CLOMP CLOMP!

King Tux dashes
behind a tall
milk can.

Mr. Grumps is
coming closer
and closer.
CLOMP CLOMP CLOMP!

But King Tux rolls into a tiny black ball. He hides his
white chest and white paws. Mr. Grumps cannot see
him in the dark shadow of the milk can.

When Mr. Grumps is far
away, King Tux uses all of his
tiny might to push the milk
can next to the barn door.

He leaps on top and stretches as high as he can.

King Tux pushes and pushes and pushes on the wooden beam that locks the barn door—without success.

"C'mon, King Tux," Scooter says from behind the door. "You can do this!"

King Tux hears Mr. Grumps' footsteps again. **CLOMP CLOMP CLOMP!** They are getting closer!

With all of his tiny might, King Tux stretches and pushes on the lock again. This time it opens!

King Tux and Scooter scamper to the far end of the farm.
They come upon a pond surrounded by soft mushy grass.

King Tux looks over this green, quiet spot hidden by Willow and Oak trees. He turns his head from side to side. He is thinking again.

"This will work," King Tux finally says. "It's not hay, but the mice can live here in comfort. Let's go get that mouse and bring her here."

Scooter runs with King Tux back to the barn.
They listen but don't hear Mr. Grumps' footsteps.

King Tux squeezes through the hole.

He runs to find the mouse and catch her in his mouth.

He carries the mouse back through hole.

The mouse is terrified! She is certain that Scooter and King Tux are going to eat her.

"Please don't eat me!" she screams. "I have a husband and children!"

"No, no, no," Scooter exclaims. Then he explains King Tux's plan and the mouse smiles.

They hear Mr. Grumps' **CLOMP CLOMP CLOMP** again.
So they dash away to the pond.

The mouse looks around the pond and squeaks with delight.

"Wow. This is nice," she says. "This will make a good home. I'll gather up all the other mice and bring them here. Thank you so much!"

Scooter and King Tux smile and say goodbye.

King Tux and Scooter run to the neighbor's house.
"Scooter, I know you will be happy here!" says King Tux.

This makes King Tux happy, too. He likes helping others.

King Tux says goodbye to Scooter and walks toward the road to Hopeville.

"Wait," Scooter shouts. "Where are you going?"

"You have your home," King Tux says.
"Now I'm going to find mine."

King Tux tells Scooter he heard a rumor at the shelter about a place called the H.O.M.E. Clinic run by a Doctor Owlkin and Nurse Sharky. "I hear they Help Or Motivate Everybody!"

Scooter waves his final goodbye and says, "That will be perfect for you. You're a smart leader who can help others."

At the cream-colored building with blue shutters near Hopeville, Doctor Owlkin, Nurse Sharky and the dog named Trouble are eating their lunch.

They hear a knock at the door.

"Nurse Sharky looks through the peep hole. No one is there.

She opens the door but still does not see anyone.

"I'm down here!" shouts tiny King Tux.

"And who might you be?" Nurse Sharky asks.

"I'm King Tux and I am here to help you,"
he says in his tiny little voice.

When Doctor Owlkin spies the little fellow, he hoots,
"Whooo do we have here?"

Nurse Sharky says, "His name is King Tux.
He is here to help us."

Trouble reaches out with her extraordinarily long ears
to give their new helper a hug.

"Welcome to the H.O.M.E. Clinic," Trouble says.
"You may be small but I can tell you are special!"

King Tux smiles. For the first time ever, he feels he is at home.

THE END

Book Three

Learn the story of the next member of
The H.O.M.E. Team
"Pirate"